Saying Goodbye

Carmel Reilly
Cheryl Orsini

Rigby

www.Rigby.com
1-800-531-5015

Rigby Focus Forward

This Edition © 2009 Rigby, a Harcourt Education Imprint

Published in 2007 by Nelson Australia Pty Ltd ACN: 058 280 149
A Cengage Learning company

All rights reserved. No part of the material protected by this copyright may be reproduced or utilized in any form or by any means, in whole or in part, without permission in writing from the copyright owner. Requests for permission should be mailed to: Paralegal Department, 6277 Sea Harbor Drive, Orlando, FL 32887.

Rigby is a trademark of Harcourt, registered in the United States of America and/or other jurisdictions.

1 2 3 4 5 6 7 8 374 14 13 12 11 10 09 08 07
Printed and bound in China

Saying Goodbye
ISBN-13 978-1-4190-3719-1
ISBN-10 1-4190-3719-6

If you have received these materials as examination copies free of charge, Rigby retains title to the materials and they may not be resold. Resale of examination copies is strictly prohibited and is illegal.

Possession of this publication in print format does not entitle users to convert this publication, or any portion of it, into electronic format.

Carmel Reilly
Cheryl Orsini

Contents

Chapter 1 **Getting Dressed Up** 4
Chapter 2 **Remembering** 6
Chapter 3 **Helping Out** 12
Chapter 4 **Saying Goodbye** 16

Getting Dressed Up

I feel really odd all dressed up.
Mom said I have to put on
my best clothes.
She said today is a big day,
and we need to look good for Grandpa.

It's funny because Grandpa never liked
getting dressed up much.
But Mom says that just for today
it's important.
So that's why I'm all dressed up.

Getting Dressed Up

Chapter 2

Remembering

I can't believe Grandpa is gone.
I keep thinking that he's going
to walk in here any time.

I can see him now.
His hair would stick up
on his head
like ice cream on top
of a cone.
I can see his brown skin,
all freckled from the sun.
I'll always remember his big smile.

Remembering

Saying Goodbye

When Grandpa was a kid,
he was good at sports.
He got lots of prizes
for all kinds of things.

When he got older,
he started playing golf.
He also got lots of prizes for golf.

Remembering

After a while,
Grandma told Grandpa
he had to stop
playing golf.
She said there was no room left
in the house
for any of her things.
But he didn't stop playing.

Saying Goodbye

Grandpa loved telling stories and jokes. He could even do magic tricks. Sometimes he would find a coin behind one of my ears.

He would laugh
as he handed the coin to me.
His thin, freckled hand
would shake just a little.

Chapter 3

Helping Out

Grandpa loved being in his garden.
He liked to hear the radio
when he worked.

Helping Out

Sometimes I'd help him.
He would tell me funny stories
about when he was a boy.
Then I'd tell him all about school
and my friends.

Saying Goodbye

Yesterday Mom and I went over
to help Grandma.
For a little while, I didn't remember
that Grandpa was gone.
I went out into the garden
to look for him.

It was so quiet.
The radio wasn't on.
Suddenly it hit me—I was never going
to see Grandpa again.

Chapter 4

Saying Goodbye

Today I am going to talk about Grandpa.
I will tell everyone about
what a good man he was.
I will tell them how much fun we had.
It's going to be hard
to say all these things,
but I think it will be good.
It will be a good way for me
to say goodbye.